GUILTY

UNTIL PROVEN **INNOCENT**

AND THINGS **NEVER** TO DO WHEN YOU ARE
SUSPECTED OF COMMITTING A CRIME

10 WAYS TO AVOID A DUI
ARREST / CONVICTION

*Dealing With the Criminal Justice
System*

By

Attorney
Vincent W. Davis

Published 2019.

Printed in the United States of America.

ISBN: 9781088947920

$16.95

Designed and published by

Vincent W. Davis
150 N. Santa Anita Avenue, Suite 200
Arcadia, CA 91706

Acknowledgments

The author wishes to thank members of his staff, past and present, who contributed to the publication of this book, and give special recognition to my deceased wife and son, Denise Doucette Davis, and my son, Vincent Clyde Davis.

Marissa Doucette Davis and I will always share the memories.

Guilty Until Proven Innocent

TABLE OF CONTENTS

INTRODUCTION

This book is written to be helpful to all citizens confronted with criminal justice issues. Charging decisions are the many important steps of the criminal justice process.

"Overcharging" to extract a plea to a lower, more appropriate charge, is not an appropriate legal tactic. Similar to threatening someone with a crime to extort a civil result (known as extortion), I believe it is an abuse of power for a prosecuting attorney to overcharge a defendant when the prosecuting attorney knows that they likely don't have enough evidence to support a conviction for the more serious charge.

Often, the prosecution will count on a defendant being intimidated into pleading to a less serious charge rather than risk going to trial. Yet some prosecutors do just that—knowingly overcharge defendants in hopes of extracting a plea to a lesser, more appropriate offense.

I realize there is a difference between strongly believing that legally admissible evidence supports a charge, and knowing that a particular jury may go either way when deciding proof beyond a reasonable doubt. The evidence submitted to the prosecutor will be the most important factor in determining whether the prosecutor brings charges, and if so, what charges. *Accordingly, it is critical to help control what evidence an accused gives to the police, whether voluntarily or otherwise.*

Aside from giving the reader of this book general knowledge about how criminal justice systems work, in general, the overarching purpose of this book is to alert citizens of actions to take and, just as importantly, actions not to take, when they become aware that they may be the subject of a police investigation where they are a suspect for committing a crime.

Under many state and federal constitutions, both prosecutors and police have broad discretionary powers. As such, both prosecutors and police occupy positions of trust. How many times is a citizen stopped and "let off" with a warning by a police officer? As a criminal law professor liked to say, "Police officers are the foot soldiers of the Constitution." Unchecked, police officers unilaterally often decide not to further investigate a person for criminal behavior, *and this is a good thing.* We trust our police officers to do the right thing, and decide when to do more than just ask questions. If every complaint of criminal behavior had to be brought to the county prosecuting attorney, we would need hundreds more prosecutors and judges to process criminal cases.

Many prosecutors and police officers are good people doing the right things, day after day and year after year. So this book has not been written out of a belief that nefarious activities are the norm when it comes to how police officers and prosecutors perform their responsibilities. Rather, to the contrary, my experience is that many prosecutors, police officers, and judges in many criminal justice systems are honest and hardworking. And, day in and day out, individuals who participate in a particular state's criminal justice system typically do the right thing when performing their respective duties. Having said that, each one of these positions has immense power, and such power left unchecked can, and from time to time, be abused.

We all hear about reports of a bad cop, a bad prosecutor, or a bad judge who was bought off or who acted out of personal bias rather than the public good when pursuing criminal charges against an individual. Sometimes it's just laziness or incompetence that leads to charges being filed, when with more careful attention being paid, such charges would have never been brought in the first place. There are also cases when witnesses lie to the police.

Many times just being charged with a crime is as harmful to the person as if he or she is actually found guilty.

This is especially true when it comes to charges that deal with moral turpitude, especially crimes with sexual connotations. The damage to a person's reputation that comes from being charged with a sexual assault is enormous. People charged with crimes involving morality issues (sexual assault, fraud, embezzlement, etc.) often entertain ideations of suicide, believing that everyone now thinks that they are guilty of doing something immoral just because charges have been brought against them.

Accordingly, charges involving morality crimes, especially charges involving sexual conduct, are some of the many serious in our society. Such charges have the potential of requiring the offender to register for life as a "sexual offender." Such labeling closes doors for life for the individual required to register as a sexual offender. In these types of cases, making sure the prosecutor has the other side's evidence (the accused) to consider *before* charges are brought is especially crucial for every potential defendant.

This book has been written to help and guide individuals who are confronted with a criminal investigation by providing information regarding what steps immediately need to be taken to make sure that the individual's account of what happened gets presented to the prosecutor at the same time the police investigative report is submitted. Often the two are not the same.

It is one thing for an individual to be represented by a competent criminal defense attorney and have the individual's information fully presented to the prosecutor, and it's quite another thing to have only the police interview the defendant, who chooses what questions to ask to illicit the initial information, and then selectively decide what portions of such an interview to present to the prosecutor. How such information is presented to the prosecutor, by the criminal law attorney, often makes a huge difference on whether the prosecutor believes that he or she has enough evidence to issue charges in a particular case.

1

THE PLAYERS IN THE CRIMINAL JUSTICE SYSTEM

Many states' criminal justice systems involve a county prosecuting official, referred to as a "county prosecutor." He or she often has one or more assistants, who have the same role and powers as the elected county prosecutor.

Within many counties, there are also prosecuting officials for cities and/or townships who enforce ordinances within their individual political subdivisions.

The prosecuting attorney, or one of his or her assistants, is the individual who makes the initial decision whether to bring criminal charges against a person. Such charges are brought, in the case of the county prosecutor, in the name of the "People of the State of . . . . ." In cases in which charges are brought by other governmental units, they are brought in the name of the "City of . . ." or "Township of . . ." City/ Township attorneys can usually only enforce criminal offenses classified as misdemeanors with a maximum punishment of approximately 93 days being spent in the local county jail. County prosecutors or their assistants, on the other hand, can usually prosecute felony charges providing for punishment of up to life in prison.

Generally the process starts when one person accuses another person of criminal behavior. The person making the accusation is known as the "complainant." Usually the complainant and the person who was wronged by the alleged criminal behavior—the "victim"—are the same person. However, sometimes the person who reports the criminal behavior is not the actual victim of the behavior. For example, sometimes the complainant is a police officer who is investigating the alleged crime, and he or she acts "upon information and belief," based on what others have told him or her when he or she filed the charges.

Guilty Until Proven Innocent

The police agency that is in charge of investigating the alleged criminal behavior depends on which agency has jurisdiction over the location where the alleged crime occurred. For example, if the crime is alleged to have occurred within the boundaries of a city, then the City Police Department will usually take the lead in the investigation. If the crime is alleged to have occurred outside an incorporated city, then usually the Sheriff's Department or the State Police (depending on who is initially called) will investigate the case.

2

THE INVESTIGATION:
WHAT TO DO IF YOU ARE A SUSPECT

After law enforcement becomes aware of the suspected crime, they begin to investigate the matter. The police investigation can involve many different techniques. Usually the police officer begins by interviewing the complainant and the alleged victim. The officer(s) may also interview other witnesses, collect physical evidence (like fingerprints, DNA, breath, or blood tests), photograph or measure the crime scene, and conduct an in-person (known as "corporeal") or photographic lineup. Generally, at some point, the investigating officer(s) will request to speak to the person who is thought to have committed the crime. This person is known as the "suspect."

Miranda Warnings

Every case is different, but it is usually not a good idea for someone suspected of committing a crime to speak to a law enforcement officer without first consulting with an experienced criminal defense attorney. There are two reasons for this. First, if the suspect is (1) in custody, and (2) being interrogated, then any statement made by the suspect is admissible in court—even a confession. If the police officer does not restrict the person's right to leave, the police officer is not required to recite the "Miranda Rights" to the suspect. Often, the police will begin their questioning by advising the person to be questioned, "You are free to leave at any time, but I would like you to help me clear up a few things."

After a person is *arrested*, however, the accused must be advised of their Miranda Rights in order for their responses to questions to be admissible in court. The Miranda decision does not require

the police to advise the arrested person of what they have

been charged with, only that any statement they make can, and will, be used against them by a court of law; that they have the right to remain silent; that they have the right to an attorney; and that their attorney may be present before answering any further questions. People often tell me, "They can't prosecute me. They never advised me of my Miranda Rights." Well, the police don't have to advise individuals of the Miranda Rights, and the issue of whether they did or did not advise a person of their Miranda Rights is only relevant in regard to the admissibility of incriminating statements alleged to have been made by an accused while in police custody.

Second, in some states, it is a crime to give information "that is false" to a "peace officer" who is conducting a criminal investigation. A "peace officer" is broadly defined and includes many law enforcement types that one might not expect would be included in the definition—such as a Department of Natural Resources (DNR) officer. A person found guilty of violating this law can be convicted of anything from a misdemeanor to a felony punishable by up to four years in prison, depending on the seriousness of the crime being investigated.

Many law prohibits not only "knowingly and willfully" making a statement to the peace officer that is false or misleading, but also "willfully conceal[ing]" by "trick, scheme, or device" material information relating to the criminal investigation.

TIP:

Some state laws could be hazardous to the well-being of an otherwise law-abiding citizen, even a person who is not a "suspect" in an ongoing criminal investigation. Therefore, in many cases it is best to <u>politely</u> decline to speak to an investigating officer until a person has a chance to consult with an experienced criminal defense attorney. Often, a person who has nothing to hide will be best served to have his or her attorney present when he or she is being interrogated by the police.

Consensual Searches

Sometimes the police will conduct an investigation under the guise of a "knock and talk," in which the officers knock on the door of a home and attempt to gain voluntary consent to enter the residence, in order to uncover criminal activity. This is common in cases in which officers are investigating nuisance parties, domestic disturbances, or drug crimes.

Under these circumstances, even when there is no illegal activity going on in the home,

It is usually best to decline to allow the officer to enter the residence without a search warrant.

If the occupants of the residence consent to the officer's entry into the residence, and the officer sees evidence of illegal activity, such as drugs in "plain view," then any and all persons inside the residence can be, and often are, charged with a crime. The police will let the prosecutor or jury figure out later who actually "owned" the drugs.

Often, when a police officer has entered a residence with the occupants' consent, the officer will then confront the occupants and request "consent" to search other areas of the residence.

It is usually advisable not to consent to this search.

This is especially true when there are several people residing in the same home, because no member of the household can be completely sure whether any other member has anything illegal in his or her area of the home. This is particularly true concerning "common areas" of the residence, such as the kitchen, living room, and spare bedrooms, because if a police officer finds evidence of illegal activity, such as drugs, in one of those areas, it is likely that all roommates will be charged with a crime.

It is almost always advisable to request that any law enforcement officer, who wants to conduct a search of a home, be required to obtain a search warrant. A search warrant may also include any vehicles or computers on the property. A search warrant is an order of the court to search a particular location and seize specific evidence of a crime. In order to obtain a warrant to search a residence, an officer must "swear out" a warrant before a neutral magistrate. This means that the officer must swear, or affirm, under oath, that there is "probable cause" to believe that evidence of a crime will be found in the location to be searched. This oath is supported by an affidavit, which lists the grounds for issuing the warrant and the alleged facts on which the probable cause finding will be based. The affidavit is usually also signed by a prosecutor. Generally the magistrate must sign the search warrant in order for it to be enforceable.

When law enforcement officials conduct a search pursuant to a search warrant, it is commonly called "executing" the warrant. The officers may seize the items specifically listed in the warrant, as well as items where it is "immediately apparent" that they are fruits, instrumentalities, contraband, or mere evidence of *other* crimes, without securing an additional search warrant. Evidence seized by law enforcement, pursuant to a search warrant, is presumed to be admissible in court, and the person charged with the crime has the burden of proving that the search was unreasonable, and therefore, the evidence must be suppressed.

An experienced criminal defense attorney will consider whether the search warrant was valid and whether the search performed by the officers was within the scope of the warrant when representing a client charged with a crime.

Sometimes law enforcement officers request voluntary consent from an individual in order to draw blood, conduct a breath test, or take DNA as evidence of a crime. Neither is it a good idea to consent to provide this evidence depending on the context in which the officer requests it.

Similarly, sometimes a police officer will stop a person on the street in order to investigate whether criminal activity is afoot. Generally this type of stop is permissible when the officer is able to refer to "articulable facts" in support of having a "reasonable suspicion" that criminal activity has happened or is about to occur. In some states, this type of stop is commonly referred to as a *Terry* stop. Often the officer will want to pat down, or "frisk," the person stopped on the street. Under the law, a frisk is only permissible if the officer has a "reasonable suspicion" that the person stopped is armed with a weapon. However, police officers often use the frisk as an opportunity to look for drugs or other contraband in a person's clothing or on his or her body.

Therefore, as discussed earlier, it is best to politely decline to speak to the officer, until the person has an opportunity to consult with an experienced criminal defense attorney. If an officer requests information as to who you are, simply provide your drivers ' license, if you have one on your person, or advise the officer of your name and address and say no more. If pressed by the officer, simply say, "Please let me call my attorney."

TIP: Discovering that you are the focus of a criminal investigation, or worse—being charged with a criminal offense—is a terrifying experience for any individual. Regardless of the charge, attempting to represent yourself, and make your way through the criminal justice system without experienced counsel, is not recommended. The simplest of assumptions and mistakes in judgment from "being too close" to the matter can haunt those caught in the criminal justice system for years after the judge drops the gavel.

From popular media, people generally know that you have the "right to remain silent." The problem is that many people are naive in terms of the goals of an investigating officer or the prosecuting official. People believe that if they "just tell the truth," or what they believe or perceive to be "the truth," then they will be believed. In short, they believe they can talk their way out of the situation.

Criminal investigators recognize, and rely, upon this thought process and will give you ample opportunity to say things that may ultimately be used against you. Quite often your words are misinterpreted by the investigator, or not properly preserved for later use. Remember, this is your only case. The officer may be working on hundreds of complaints a month and may not accurately remember what you explained days or weeks after your interview. If you are contacted by the police, and they attempt to question you or a loved one, contact an attorney immediately. Generally, as previously discussed, unless you have been placed in police custody, the investigator is not required to advise you of your rights to have an attorney present during any questioning.

You are never under any obligation to speak to police. Know your rights. Exercise them and advise the investigator that you wish to consult an attorney before answering any questions.

The investigator may attempt to tell you that asking to speak to an attorney will only hurt your position with the prosecutor, or that the attorney will only advise you to not make a statement. Trust us when we say that no ethical prosecuting official will hold it against you for wanting to speak to an attorney before answering questions. Be firm and respectful to the investigator and clearly advise him or her that you wish to consult with an attorney before answering any questions.

If you are charged with a crime, having an attorney represent you throughout the proceedings is crucial.

This is true whether you've been charged with a misdemeanor or a felony. Minor offenses can have a devastating effect on your life, family, and career. Simply pleading guilty to a "minor offense" without the advice of counsel **"just to get it over with" can have severe future consequences. Alcohol offenses or minor drug possession convictions can impact your driver's license, even if you weren't driving at the time of the incident. Violations of the motor vehicle code can never be expunged! The stigma of having a fraud or theft conviction, such as "shoplifting," has far-reaching effects, and the law allows your credibility in the future to be attacked for these types of offenses. Don't let your or your children's "minor mistake" damage your or their reputation or career.**

If you or someone you love has been contacted by the police to give a statement, my recommendation is to first take the time to discuss the matter with an experienced criminal defense attorney. You have no legal obligation to answer questions or give a statement. Protect your interests by advising the police that you wish to consult with an attorney first.

DNA Tests

In some types of cases, such as alleged criminal sexual conduct matters, police officers may request that a person

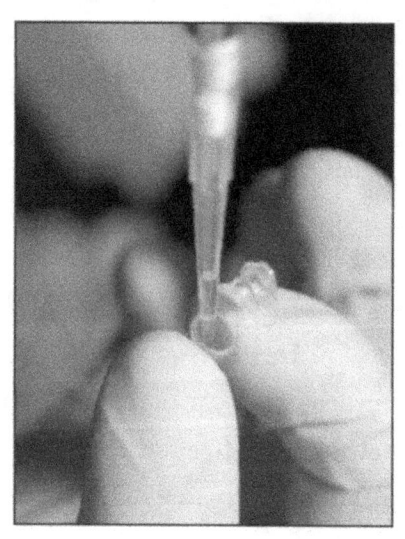

voluntarily submit to DNA testing. DNA testing can be as simple as swabbing the inside of a person's cheek.

It is never a good idea to submit to DNA testing voluntarily.

Once a person's DNA is collected, and submitted to law enforcement, in many cases, it will remain in the public domain indefinitely.

Polygraphs

In many states, polygraph examinations are used by both law enforcement and criminal defense attorneys. A polygraph, otherwise  known as a "lie detector," consists of connecting the person to be tested via rubber tubes and metal plates to the polygraph machine. The machine collects physiological data from the subject's respiratory system, sweat glands, and cardiovascular system.

Although common wisdom holds that polygraph results are not admissible in court, in reality, whether a court will consider them depends on the individual court and the reason for which they are being used.

Generally, it is not a good idea to participate in a polygraph examination without first consulting with an experienced criminal defense attorney.

For example, in many states, upon request, a person charged with criminal sexual conduct has the absolute right to a polygraph examination by a law enforcement agency upon request. In practice, however, it is not uncommon for someone who is being truthful not to pass the test. In fact, an "inconclusive" result often will occur even when someone is telling the truth. This happens as much as 20 percent of the time. Therefore, a criminal defense attorney may request that his or her client participate in a polygraph examination by a private (i.e., not law enforcement) examiner *prior* to submitting to one to be performed by the police.

Statements made to the polygraph examiner by the person taking the test, generally are considered privileged. This is especially true when an attorney requests that his or her client participate in a polygraph exam. This means that the polygrapher may not disclose the statements to a third party. However, when a person is taking a polygraph at the request of law enforcement, such as in a criminal sexual conduct investigation, that person cannot reasonably expect that his statements will make it into the hands of the police.

Sometimes, an experienced criminal defense attorney will request that his or her client submit to a polygraph examination, in order to strengthen the client's position with the prosecutor. For example, if the client has passed the polygraph exam, a persuasive attorney may be able to convince the prosecutor not to issue charges in the first place (i.e., his word against hers) or to dismiss the charges that have been filed against the client.

Police officers often request that persons suspected of committing crimes participate in an in-person identification. The identification is designed to allow a crime victim, or a person who witnesses a crime, to identify the alleged perpetrator. An in-person identification can happen in two ways: at the scene of an alleged crime (a one-person "show-up"), or at a police station (a multiple-person "lineup"). Generally, a person suspected of a crime is entitled to be represented by an attorney at an identification only after criminal proceedings against that person have started.

In general, again it is not advisable to participate in an in-person identification without first consulting with an attorney.

3

SUSPECTED OF
DRIVING UNDER THE INFLUENCE (DUI)

Police officers often stop automobiles in order to investigate potential criminal activity. This is particularly true of suspected drunk driving or drug possession cases. When the law enforcement officer stops the vehicle, the police officer often indicates to the driver that the stop was made because of a traffic violation (weaving across traffic, failing to come to a complete stop, etc.) or faulty vehicle equipment, when the officer's true intent may have been actually to investigate another suspected crime. Believe it or not, this type of stop, known as a "pretextual stop," is perfectly legal. During this stop, the officer may detain the vehicle and its passengers for the amount of time reasonably necessary to control the scene and accomplish the purpose of the stop (e.g., to write a traffic ticket). The officer may also run the driver's and passengers' criminal background checks (in some areas, this is known to law enforcement as LEIN) during the stop in order to, among other things, see if there are any outstanding arrest warrants. *It is also permissible for the officer to ask that the occupants of the vehicle to exit the automobile.*

During the automobile stop, the police officer often will ask to search the inside of the vehicle and its contents (including backpacks, purses, etc.).

Usually, it is best not to consent to a search of a vehicle.

This is true especially if there are other occupants in the vehicle, because it is very difficult to be sure that no one in the automobile has anything illegal (contraband) with them inside of it. It is important to note that, *even without consent,* the police officer may search a vehicle without a search warrant, based on a specific exception in the law that covers automobiles. However, the "automobile exception" still requires that the officer have probable cause to believe that evidence of criminal activity will be found in the vehicle. Once the officer determines that probable cause exists to search the vehicle, the officer can search all of the backpacks, purses, etc., that are found within the automobile.

It is important to note that if the occupants of the vehicle don't consent to the vehicle search, and the officer searches it anyway and finds evidence of criminal activity (such as drugs), an experienced criminal defense attorney can argue to the judge that the evidence should be suppressed, because there was no probable cause for the search at the time that it was conducted. If consent was given for the search, however, the argument becomes much more difficult to make.

If an occupant of the vehicle is arrested, a police officer may search the vehicle, pursuant to the "search incident to arrest doctrine," only when (1) the arrestee is unsecured and within reaching distance of the passenger compartment at the time of the search, or (2) the officer believes that evidence related to the crime for which the person is being arrested may be found within the vehicle. When a vehicle is impounded after the arrest, so long as the officer is following the standard inventory procedure utilized by the law enforcement agency, the officer may search the vehicle in order to document everything that is found within the vehicle. This includes opening containers, the glove box, and packages found within the vehicle. During this "inventory search," if the officer finds evidence of a crime, such as drugs or a weapon, any and all occupants of the vehicle can potentially be charged with a crime.

Field Sobriety Tests

Many times when a police officer stops a vehicle driven by a suspected drunk driver, the officer will ask that the driver step out of the car in order to perform roadside field sobriety tests, also known in some areas as "FSTs." The National Highway Traffic Safety Administration (NHTSA), an agency of the Department of Transportation, recognizes three performance tests to be scientifically valid indicators of intoxication. Those performance tests are: Horizontal Gaze Nystagmus (HGN), Walk-and-Turn, and One-Leg Stand. Occasionally a police officer will request that the driver perform a different test, such as reciting the alphabet or counting backwards. However, there is less scientific evidence that supports those tests as being true indicators of a person being legally drunk, as they tend to be very subjective.

1-888-888-6582

An officer administering the HGN test is looking for nystagmus, an involuntary jerking or bouncing of the eyeball, which occurs when there is a disturbance of the inner ear (vestibular) system or the oculomotor control of the eye. In the drunk driving context, alcohol consumption is thought to hinder the ability of the brain to correctly control eye muscles, therefore causing a "jerking" or "bouncing" movement associated with HGN.

In order to administer the HGN test, the officer asks the driver to follow an object with his or her eyes, such as a pen or the tip of a penlight. The officer places the object about 12 to 15 inches from the driver's face and slightly higher than the driver's eye level. The officer then instructs the driver to keep his or her head still, while the officer moves the object side to side and up and down in front of the driver's face. The officer watches to see whether the driver's eyes smoothly follow the object, or whether there is nystagmus present.

When a police officer administers the "walk-and-turn" and "one-leg stand" tests, the officer is checking to see whether the driver can listen to and follow instructions while performing simple physical movements. The theory is that many people who are not impaired by alcohol can easily perform such tests because they don't have trouble dividing their attention between physical and mental tasks.

In the walk- and- turn test, the officer instructs the driver to take nine steps, heel to toe, along a straight line.

Suspected of Driving Under the Influence

After taking the steps, the driver must then turn on one foot and return in the same manner in the opposite direction. For the one-leg stand test, the driver is instructed to stand with one foot approximately six inches off the ground and count out loud (one thousand one, one thousand two, etc.), until he or she is told to put the foot down. The driver is told to do this for 30 seconds.

Generally, a police officer requests that a driver submit to FSTs in order to establish reasonable cause to believe that a person's ability to operate a vehicle was affected by the consumption of alcohol. Once the officer determines that reasonable cause exists, many state laws allow the officer to ask the driver to submit to a preliminary breath test, also known as a "PBT," at the scene.

MY GENERAL ADVICE:

DO NOT PARTICIPATE IN TAKING THESE TESTS!!

It is important to note that some state laws do not require a driver to participate in field sobriety tests. *They are completely voluntary.* Moreover, for a variety of reasons, including nervousness, many people fail these tests, and a driver's poor performance on them is admissible in court as proof that the driver was, in fact, driving under the influence of an intoxicating substance.

30   1-888-888-6582

For this reason, it is not usually advisable to take these tests. It must be noted, however, that the failure to participate in these tests raises a potential concern. Not agreeing to perform a field sobriety test will, at a minimum, usually lead to the police officer requesting the driver to submit to a PBT (Preliminary Breath Test). Unless dealing with a driver who is under the age of 21, prior to making such a request, the law requires that the police officer must have reasonable cause to believe the driver is affected by consumption of alcohol, controlled substances, or both. That being said, a driver's refusal to agree to perform the requested field sobriety test will typically create agitation with the police officer and, with or without the results of any PBT, there is concern that this agitation will lead to the arrest of the driver. While this should not be the case, human behavior (on the police officer's part) often dictates that an agitated police officer who is not pleased with a driver's refusal to participate in field sobriety tests and/or refusal to take a requested PBT may decide "to just arrest the driver."

The PBT

For these reasons, making the decision whether to decline to take the PBT is a slightly more difficult one. A PBT is administered by using a small, handheld device that measures breath

alcohol through a fuel cell, an ALCO-Sensor. Although, in many cases, the driver's PBT result cannot be admitted into evidence in trial as proof of a driver's intoxication, a police officer can arrest the driver based in whole, or in part, on the driver's PBT results. Refusing to take a PBT, so long as the driver is over the age of 21 and not driving a commercial motor vehicle, is a civil infraction and carries no driver's license points. Therefore, in many cases, it's generally best to refuse to submit to a PBT.

The Breath Analyzer

The many important tool used by law enforcement officers in the investigation of a driver suspected of being drunk from using alcohol is the breath analyzer. A breath analyzer is a rectangular box that measures the amount of alcohol from a driver's breath by using infrared absorption in order to measure the amount of ethanol in the driver's deep lung air. This type of chemical testing is generally considered scientifically valid. As opposed to a PBT, which is activated at the scene of the traffic stop, a police officer will only request that a driver submit to a breath analyzer testing *after arrest*, and usually at a jail or a police station.

Implied Consent Law

Under many states' "Implied Consent" statute, a driver who refuses to submit to chemical testing after an arrest will lose his or her driver's license for one year. A second or subsequent refusal within seven years will result in a two-year suspension. Additionally, six points are entered onto the driver's driving record. An appeal of the Implied Consent violation is reviewable in many states, but the only matters at issue in the Implied Consent hearing are the following:

1. Did the police officer have reasonable grounds to believe that the driver committed a crime listed in the drunk driving statute?

2. Was the driver placed under arrest for a crime listed in the drunk driving statute?

3. Did the driver refuse to submit to a chemical test requested by the officer?

4. Was the driver advised of his or her chemical test rights, as required by law?

Unless the driver can establish at the hearing that he or she meets one or more grounds or exceptions set forth above, the driver's review will not be successful, and the driver will lose his or her license for one year. A first Implied Consent suspension can be amended to include a restricted license, but only by a Circuit Court Order upon showing a hardship.

Keep in mind that the courts have found that it is reasonable to refuse to submit to a breath analyzer test if the driver asks to call an attorney prior to taking the test and is denied a reasonable opportunity to do so. Practically speaking, if the driver is pulled over at 2 o'clock in the morning, he or she is not likely to be able to consult with an attorney before submitting to the test. However, the police are obliged to let the driver try. It may be advisable to refuse to submit to a breath analyzer test if the driver has explicitly requested to consult with an attorney and has been explicitly denied the opportunity to do so. Nevertheless, it is important to keep in mind that if the driver refuses to submit to a breath analyzer, the police officer will likely seek to obtain a search warrant for a blood draw of the driver's blood anyway.

First-time Implied Consent offenders can petition the circuit court for a restricted license. It is important to note that, in many states, the Implied Consent violation is separate from the criminal drunk driving charge. Therefore, it is possible for a person to be found "not guilty" of drunk driving, but still lose his driver's license for one year, because of an Implied Consent refusal.

4

10 WAYS TO AVOID DUI ARREST AND/OR CONVICTION

(If You Have Recently Consumed Any Amount of Alcohol, or Recently Used a Controlled Substance)

1. When stopped by the police for an apparent civil infraction (e.g., speeding, crossing the centerline, etc.), *politely* respond to any request by a police officer who asks you to produce your driver's license, your motor vehicle registration, and your proof of insurance. Once you have given those documents to the police officer,

that's all you have to do or say. Thereafter, <u>politely</u> decline to have any discussion, whatsoever, with the police officer who stopped you. You have a constitutional right not to incriminate yourself when being questioned about whether you have violated the law. The Fifth Amendment to our United States Constitution includes your absolute right to remain silent, but you *must* invoke it. In many states, court decisions indicate that your mere silence can be held against you unless you explicitly and unequivocally *state words to the effect, "I invoke my constitutional right to remain silent" and "I wish to have an attorney present with me if you wish to ask me any further questions."* Having said this, again remember to remain polite with the law enforcement officer questioning you. Use terms such as "respectfully" and "please understand." After providing this information (i.e., proof of insurance, driver's license, and registration), any further conversation on your part will usually lead to trouble rather than avoiding problems.

Keep in mind that many states have a law that makes it a separate crime to conceal any material facts from a police officer conducting a criminal investigation. If you keep talking, and say something that is not true or leave out a material fact, you risk violating the statute.

2. *When being questioned, never use inappropriate or foul language.* Although you may be upset at being stopped, whatever you say can be used against you in a subsequent DUI trial. Never admit to drinking alcohol or to using any type of drugs within the last 24 hours prior to driving; simply decline to answer such questions. I continue to be amazed at the number of times that individuals get into trouble by answering questions such as: "Is there anything in your car that I need to know about? Do you have any type of drugs in this car?" Sadly, many a Michigan citizen will reply, "Yes, officer, I have a small amount of marijuana in my trunk." Unbelievable, but true. Without question, such a reply gives the police officer probable cause to search your vehicle, and likely you will be arrested for possession of marijuana. Simply say, "I do not want to answer any questions without first consulting with an attorney. I do not consent to any searches of my vehicle without a search warrant."

3. *Refuse to take any standard field sobriety tests (SFST).* Standard field sobriety tests allow police officers to subjectively determine whether you have "failed" a test. Rarely does taking field sobriety test help the police officer to decide not to charge you, whereas the opposite often occurs. SFSTs include such tests as walking a straight line, performing the

Nystagmus test, reciting the alphabet forward or backwards (without singing), counting backwards from 31 and stopping at 17, standing on one leg, and touching your nose. My advice is to simply advise the police officer that you respectfully decline to take such tests: "I've been advised by friends that I have the right to refuse to take such tests and I'm worried about how my nervousness may affect how I perform on these tests"; "I know you're just trying to do your job, officer, but I don't want to take any of these tests and I respectfully decline to do so." As of the date of authoring this book, and a review of cases in many states, there are no cases requiring you to submit to any of these types of roadside tests. If you are not arrested by the police officer after your refusal to participate in field sobriety tests, my suggestion is to tell the officer, "It's been a tough night and I 'm just going to call it a night and call a cab or a friend to come and pick me up." My advice would be to lock your car up and start walking home.

4. *Consider refusing to take a roadside preliminary breath test (PBT).* Unlike other field sobriety tests that require your physical or mental participation, a PBT is administered by a small handheld device that you blow into. If you refuse to take a PBT on the roadside, you will be charged with a civil

Guilty Until Proven Innocent

infraction and receive a fine typically ranging from $100–$200. There is no mandatory driver's license sanction for refusing a PBT, nor is your refusal to take a PBT typically admissible in any subsequent trial for DUI. My suggestion is, again, be polite and advise the police officer that even though you've refused to take the PBT, you don't believe you've done anything wrong. But if the officer believes that you have committed some civil infraction, such as speeding, then say, "Please write me a ticket and I'll be happy to address that, but I'd like to get going." It's at this point that the officer will have to make a decision whether he or she "has articulable facts" to support arresting you for DUI. Hopefully that is not the case, but if it is the case, and you are arrested, different rules apply.

5.   If you are *arrested* for a DUI:

   a.   If the police have requested you to take a breath analyzer test, and the breath analyzer test results come back and either show a 0.00 or a low number like .03 or .05, *do not agree to take any second test requested by the police officer.* After you have taken a breath analyzer test that was requested by the police, you can legally refuse to take any further testing. Sometimes the arresting officer will request that you take a different second test based on a low result from the breath analyzer test, purportedly "just to make sure that the test was operating properly." *Don't agree to take a different second test (like a blood or urine test)*; just say no.

b. *After being arrested, remember to remain silent.* Typically, everything in a police car is recorded, and everything at the jail is recorded when you are being booked. How you conduct yourself, and what you say after you have been arrested, could make a difference should you have a basis for going to trial to contest your DUI charge.

c. If you are arrested for DUI, and you are requested to take a chemical test, then under many states' implied consent law, if you do not take the requested chemical test (i.e., a breath analyzer) test at the jail or a blood or urine test at the hospital), then you face the loss of your driver's license for a period of one year. Refusing to take a requested chemical test *after* being arrested is completely different than refusing to take the preliminary breath test during the roadside interview with the police officer *before* being arrested. A PBT test is inherently unreliable, and that is why the results of a PBT test are not admissible in a trial. On the other hand, the results of a breath analyzer, blood alcohol, or urine analysis are much more reliable and hence are admissible in a subsequent DUI trial. Many states' legislatures have made it mandatory that when you drive on a public highway or place open to the public, you "implied consent" to take whatever chemical test is requested by a police officer *after* the officer has made up his or her mind to arrest you on an DUI charge. Since the sanctions are so high for refusing such a test (loss of driving privileges for one year), *I typically recommend that a first-time DUI offender take the requested chemical test.*

6. If the officer has decided to arrest you, because he or she smelled alcohol on your breath and, even though you haven't performed any sobriety tests, perhaps your speech was slurred, remember that you will be advised of your rights to take one of the chemical tests chosen by the police officer. After you have taken the test chosen by the police officer (i.e., a breath analyzer or blood test), *remember that you*

have the right to have a second independent test performed on your own. If you've taken a blood test, you can request to be taken to a police station nearby and have a breath analyzer test. If you've taken a breath analyzer test, you can request to be taken to the hospital and take a blood test. If you've taken a blood test at one hospital, you can ask to be taken to another nearby hospital and take a second blood test. The cost for the second test will have to be borne by you, but you have the right to take a second independent test of your choosing.

7. If you've been arrested by a police officer, you have the right to contact your attorney. Ask to call your attorney, and use a landline to call them. *The police are required to allow you one phone call to your attorney.* You may request to talk to your attorney at the roadside as well. "Look officer, I appreciate what you're trying to do, but I'm very nervous about this whole process, and I'm invoking my right against self-incrimination, and I'd like to talk to my attorney at this time." *If the police officer does not allow you the opportunity to call your attorney, your refusal to take the requested chemical test may not result in the loss of your driving privileges.*

8. QUESTION: What's your advice about getting out of the vehicle after being stopped by a police officer?

ANSWER: Initially, many police officers do not want you to get out of the vehicle. Rightfully, they are concerned about their own safety, and they have to make sure who they are dealing with before going further with their investigation. They will approach the vehicle and ask for your driver's license, proof of insurance, and registration. Have those items easily accessible to you in your car so you can hand them over to the officer immediately. If the officer asks you to get out of the vehicle, politely advise the officer that you prefer not to exit your vehicle, because you're concerned about your own safety. If the officer asks whether you have been drinking, used any drugs, or have anything in the car that he or she should know about, simply state, "Officer, I prefer not to discuss anything and to remain silent in regard to any of the questions that you have asked, and I am invoking my right to have an attorney present here if you wish to question me further." Remember, it is now a crime to conceal from a police officer any material fact when the police are considering a criminal investigation. *If, however, the officer orders you to get out of the vehicle and opens the door, under many states' current law, you have no choice but to comply and get out of your motor vehicle.*

Once you are outside of your vehicle, however, my advice is to remain standing immediately next to your car. If the officer says, "Come right over here. I'd like you to perform some tests," just say, "Sir, as I've indicated for my own personal safety, I do not wish to move any further away from my car. If I've done something wrong, and you have a basis for writing me a ticket, please do so, but I've gotten out of the car at your request, and I don't want to walk any further than right where I'm at. I'm nervous, I'm upset (and you are probably both), and I'm invoking my right to remain silent, and I wish to have no further questioning of me. If I've done something wrong, please write me a ticket for my civil infraction because I'd like to get moving. *I'm not willing to participate in any field sobriety tests.*" **NOTE:** I am mindful that this type of discussion may lead to irritating the police officer, even though it should not, and it may lead to the police officer making a quick snap decision to arrest you. If you have been drinking alcohol, you need to remember that performing field sobriety tests and taking a PBT *almany always will work against you in the long run, and therefore your polite refusal to take such tests is still the best advice I can give you.*

9. QUESTION: I've been involved in an accident, what are my responsibilities?

ANSWER: In many states, your responsibilities are to stop at the scene of an accident, and give the other driver your name, address, and proof of insurance. You are to exchange such information at the scene of the accident. Once you have exchanged that information, my suggestion is that you depart as soon as possible. *There is no requirement that you remain at the scene until a police officer arrives. Once you've exchanged the required information (name, address, and proof of insurance) with the other driver, you can leave.* If you have been drinking any amount of alcohol or used any illegal drugs within 24 hours of this accident, once you've exchanged the required information with the other driver, my suggestion is to depart from the scene; either walk away, call a cab, or call a friend to come and have you picked up. I make this statement assuming that no one is left at the scene injured or needing medical assistance. If that is the case, obviously you should call 911 and request medical assistance.

If your vehicle has struck another vehicle, and there is no individual around, my advice is to leave your name and insurance information under the windshield wiper of the vehicle struck and, again, for safety purposes, leave the scene of the accident. Thereafter, my advice is to notify the police of this accident. Many states require that there be "police contact forthwith," Also, many states have statutes that require *any* injury or damage to an apparent extent of $1,000 be reported to the police.

10. QUESTION: If, while driving, I observe a police officer traveling behind me at a slow rate of speed, and I'm worried that I may be stopped, what should I do?

ANSWER: My advice is *not to stop your vehicle* unless, and until, the officer's overhead lights are activated, or a siren is activated signaling you to stop. Obviously, until stopped, continue within the speed limit and obey all traffic laws and signal for all turns, even if it's a minor lane change, and do not do anything additional to attract the attention of the officer. As long as your vehicle continues moving, the police are not entitled to stop your vehicle without a valid reason. The police must determine that there was a traffic violation committed by you. If you stop your vehicle, however, under a Supreme Court decision (*Terry v Ohio*, 392 US 1 [1968]), "The police are entitled to approach your vehicle and question you to determine whether criminal activity is afoot." This is often the time when incriminating evidence is passed on to the police regarding your previous use of alcohol or drugs.

5

RETAINED EXPERTS PROVE OUR CLIENTS' INNOCENCE

Case 1

One of my clients came to me charged with setting fire to the family home he inherited after the death of his parents. The insurance company insuring the home had encouraged local police and fire department personnel to pursue an arson case against my client, because the insurance investigator didn't think things looked right *and* they didn't like the answers my client gave them.

Retained Experts Proved our Clients' Innocence

The next thing my client knew, the local police had brought in representatives of the United States Department of Justice—a federal law enforcement organization known as the Bureau of Alcohol, Tobacco, Firearms and Explosives (BATFE). The experts claimed that my client had set a time-sensitive explosive device to blow up when he wasn't there, and which caused the fire.

The police theorized that my client's inherited home had been listed "for sale" for two years, with no sale, and he wanted to burn it for the insurance proceeds.

After I was retained, I filed motions to get the "explosive device" that had been examined released, and had the remains of what was left (after the fire) sent to our retained Forensic Laboratory Experts. After our experts examined the explosive device, microscopic serial numbers were uncovered, which concluded that the explosive device was, in fact, a smoke alarm built in the 1950's!

After disclosing that the explosive bomb was actually a smoke detector, criminal charges were dismissed. I then sued the insurance company for my client's fire loss of his home. I also sought what is known as "exemplary damages" for the outrageous conduct of representatives of my client's insurance company, who turned against their own insured and tried to get him convicted of a crime he had not committed. Months later, I obtained a six-figure financial settlement for all claims.

1-888-888-6582

What this case illustrates is the importance of hiring an experienced team of criminal defense attorneys to represent an accused, early on, so that evidence can be tested. The decision to procure the remains of "the explosive device", and have the same "independently tested", made the criminal difference in proving our client's innocence. The ATF expert testified at the preliminary examination that he had examined all possible known devices available to consumers, and this device "was not available anywhere to members of the public." The "so-called expert" testified that the remains of a melted circuit board was "an explosive incendiary device"—a bomb—set to explode by a timer that had burned and been consumed in the fire.

Talk about having egg on your face, the embarrassed "expert" purportedly apologized to my client when the serial numbers conclusively proved that "the explosive device" was actually a smoke detector. Thousands of dollars later, the "apology" helped little after my client had his reputation in the community tarnished and spent time at the local jail being referred to as an alleged felon. Yes, the police had him "guilty" *until* we proved his innocence!

Case 2

Another client of our firm was involved in a motor vehicle accident where a young boy was killed. In that accident, the truck my client was driving came into contact with the bicycle the boy was riding. Initially the police believed the truck ran into the boy's bicycle, as the boy was riding to school at approximately 7:30 a.m. to 8:00 a.m.

My client was charged with negligent homicide. He was also later sued by the child's estate for the child's wrongful death.

After reading the police report, and talking with my client, I retained the experts I cite below),

I had one picture in my mind as to how the accident had occurred. The picture in my mind wasn't one that I felt would help my client under the circumstances.

Again, things aren't always as they appear. I immediately sought help from the services of an experienced independent accident reconstruction expert. I also retained the services of a conspicuity expert. A conspicuity expert is an expert in a subspecialty field of psychology who can offer opinion testimony as to why people see or do not see something before them. A conspicuity expert would be able to possibly help me explain why my client was not able to see the boy on the bicycle who was riding on or near the edge of the highway prior to the accident.

After the evidence was examined by the experts, and after their opinions were shared with me, a much different picture emerged of what had happened (and yes, more importantly, what had *not* happened).

1-888-888-6582

Picture Before Experts Were Retained

Picture After Experts Were Retained

The above facts painted quite a different picture of the accident scene. Added to this picture was a set of oncoming headlights of the vehicle cresting the hill from the northbound lane, which was veering towards the centerline

1-888-888-6582

after cresting (per the testimony of a 16-year-old driver who stated that she "always pulled over to the right" as she approached a hill, and once she crested the hill, she drove back left towards the center of the road).

This 16-year-old's testimony allowed the conspicuity expert to testify at court that the oncoming truck driver's eyes would have been "focused," out of fear, to a 5 percent degree of acuity, on the headlights of the car coming toward his lane. The cumulative effect of the truck driver focusing on the approaching danger of the vehicle moving toward the center of the roadway (and towards his lane of travel), together with the lack of any visibility or contrast on the part of the bicyclist, provided the foundation for the conspicuity expert, testifying at trial, that there was "no way possible" that the truck driver ever saw, or more importantly, *could have* even seen the bicyclist, prior to impact.

The accident reconstruction expert also testified that, based on how the accident was documented, there was no way to tell whether it was the bicyclist who had actually turned into the path of the truck driver.

It was also the accident reconstruction expert who discovered that workers for the county road commission had mismarked the centerline on the roadway. This caused the southbound traveled portion (between the white lines marking each outer edge of the northbound and southbound lanes) to be only nine feet wide, when it should have been 10 feet wide. Considering the fact that the truck was eight feet, six inches wide, the extra 12 inches not available for driving was likely a critical factor contributing to the cause of this tragic accident.

The conspicuity expert and I traveled to the sheriff's department and photographed the clothing that had been worn by the deceased boy at the time of the accident. The conspicuity expert used equipment to measure the clothing's light absorption factor versus its light reflecting factor. The dark clothes also exacerbated the lack of contrast that naturally occurs in early morning light. Making visibility matters worse, there was also a light mist in the air.

The accident reconstruction expert also went to the sheriff's department and examined the damaged bicycle that the young boy was riding at the time of the accident. Sadly, it was determined that when someone assembled the bike, or maintained the bike, they inadvertently turned the rear reflector upside down: it was positioned below the seat and *below* the rear fender, so it would not have been visible to reflect light that came from behind the bicycle.

Had these two experts not been retained to develop the evidence that was there to be developed (but had not been developed during the police investigation), there is no doubt in my mind that an innocent man would have been convicted of a crime that he did not commit.

The jury took less than one hour to return a "not guilty" verdict against my client. Had my client been convicted, he would have lost his job as a state building inspector who traveled to construction sites throughout the state to evaluate compliance with construction contracts, which would have been a devastating financial loss. Had he been convicted, he would have been wrongfully labeled a criminal and likely spent six months to a year in jail as punishment for his crime of negligent homicide.

Coincidentally, the evidence gathered to protect my client from being wrongfully convicted of a crime also provided potential evidence to assist the estate of the deceased boy in pursuing a third-party negligence claim against the county road commission for mismarking the roadway where the accident occurred.

The bottom line: Justice can be better served by taking quick action to contact an experienced criminal defense attorney to preserve and develop evidence. Employing accident reconstruction experts, biomechanical experts, and motor vehicle experts, such as the air brake expert and a conspicuity expert, can determine whether you will be found guilty for a crime as serious as vehicle man-slaughter or negligent homicide.

6

COMMON CRIMINAL CHARGES

There are hundreds of crimes with which people can be charged. However, below are the charges that I encounter many often in my criminal law practice.

Assaultive Crimes

Disorderly Person

This is not technically an assault, but it is commonly used as a lesser offense to plead to when a person is charged with an assaultive crime. A person is guilty of "jostling" , under the disorderly person statute, if that person "jostl[es]" or is "roughly crowding people unnecessarily in a public place". In many states, a disorderly person "jostling" is a misdemeanor punishable by up to 90 days in jail and a fine of up to $500.

In many states, the "disorderly person" statute, is entertaining and worth reviewing. It criminalizes such behavior as being a "common prostitute," a "window peeper," and "begging."

Assault / Assault and Battery

An assault is *either* (1) an attempt to commit a battery (to cause physical harm), or (2) an unlawful act that places another person in reasonable *apprehension* of receiving an immediate battery. A battery is a completed assault. A common question asked of criminal defense attorneys is, "How can I be charged with assault, when I didn't touch him (or her)?" Under many state laws, a person can be convicted of assault by simply attempting to batter another person, or by putting that person *in fear* of being battered. It is not necessary to prove that an actual physical touch occurred. In many states, an assault, or an assault and battery, is a misdemeanor punishable by up to 93 days in jail and a fine of not more than $500.

Domestic Violence

An assault, or assault and battery, constitutes domestic violence when the victim of the crime is the defendants' spouse or former spouse, an individual with whom he or she has or has had a dating relationship, an individual with whom he or she has had a child in common, or a resident or former resident of his or her household." In many states, domestic violence is a misdemeanor punishable by up to 93 days in jail or a fine of not more than $500. A *second conviction* for domestic violence is a misdemeanor punishable by up to one year in jail and a fine of not more than $1,000. A *third conviction* for domestic violence is a *felony* punishable by imprisonment for not more than five years and a fine of up to $5,000.

There is a deferral program available for persons convicted of domestic violence for the first time. If a defendant who is placed on deferral status with the court (sometimes known as a "Section 796.4a deferral" or "domestic violence deferral") successfully completes probation, then the defendant's case can be dismissed and no public conviction is entered onto his or her record. However, many states' laws have been amended to stipulate that a prior successful domestic violence deferral can still be used as a predicate basis for a "second" or "third" offense domestic enhancement in the future.

I have tried many domestic violence cases and, as of the date of publishing this book, I have won every case. I recommend that you never take a deferral, unless you believe you physically abused a domestic partner. If someone shoved you, and/or you shoved him/her back, in many states, that is not the type of "domestic violence" that a jury will convict you for under domestic violence statutes.

Aggravated Assault

Aggravated assault is an assault and battery without a weapon in which the offender inflicts a serious or aggravated injury on the complainant. Whether an injury is serious or aggravated, is a question of fact that is context- specific. Additionally, the prosecutor does not need an expert witness to testify that the injury was serious or aggravated in order to convince a jury of that fact. In many states, aggravated assault is punishable by up to one year imprisonment and a fine of not more than $1,000—MCL 750.81a.

Felonious Assault

A felonious assault is an assault that occurs with a dangerous weapon. Whether an instrument constitutes a "dangerous weapon", for the purposes of the statute, is a question of fact for the jury and is very case-specific. For example, an operable, though unloaded, pellet gun has been found to constitute a "dangerous weapon," as has an aerosol spray can, beer bottle, and broomstick. In many states, a felonious assault is a felony punishable by up to four years imprisonment and a fine of up to $2,000.

Assault with Intent to Do Great Bodily Harm Less than Murder

This is an assault of an attempted or a completed battery in which the defendant had the intent to do serious injury of an aggravated nature, or in which the defendant committed an assault "by strangulation or suffocation." A great bodily harm assault is a high-severity felony, punishable by up to 10 years in prison and a fine of up to $5,000.

In my experience, this crime is many often charged as a "lesser-included" offense, along with murder or attempted murder. However, in cases in which the alleged assault has caused serious injuries to the victim, or appears extremely egregious, assault with intent to do great bodily harm is charged as the more serious count, together with the lesser assaults that I have already discussed. Additionally, the legislature recently amended the great bodily harm statute to include assaults by strangulation or suffocation, so I expect to see prosecutors issue more great bodily harm charges in the future.

Resisting and Obstructing a Police Officer

Generally, anyone who "assaults, batters, wounds, resists, obstructs, opposes, or endangers a person who the individual knows, or has reason to know, is performing his or her duties, is guilty of a felony punishable by imprisonment for not more than two years or a fine of not more than $2,000 or both." If the "resistance" and "obstruction" causes a *physical injury* to the officer, then it is a felony punishable by up to four years imprisonment and a fine of up to $5,000. In many states, if a *"serious impairment of a body function"* occurs, then it is a felony punishable by up to 15 years in prison or a fine of up to $10,000 or both.

The "resisting and obstructing" crime is not limited to acts involving police officers. Therefore, a person can be charged under this statute for "resisting" any person who is "performing his or her duties." Conceivably, this includes meter attendants and mall security guards.

Also, in many cases, it does not matter whether the "individual performing his or her duties" is a police officer making an illegal arrest at the time that the defendant resists or obstructs the officer. Therefore, with limited exceptions, it is not permissible to use force to resist an illegal arrest. In addition, resisting does not require physical force by the defendant, and intoxication is not a defense to this crime. I took a case all the way to a high Court to win a case for my client where the prosecutor charged my client with "obstructing the police" by lying to the police regarding his name. The prosecutor argued that the phrase "resisting and

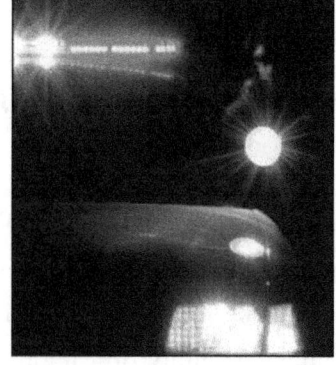

obstructing" also meant impeding a police investigation by slowing down the investigative process by misleading the police as to my client's name. In a 4–3 decision, the high court agreed with my position that "the obstructing phrase" had to be read together with the other words of the statute that meant "a physical obstruction," such as "getting in the way" of the police trying to execute a lawful command, such as a search warrant.

Drunk or Drugged Driving Crimes

In many states, drunk driving laws are one of the many complicated and misunderstood criminal statutes in the state. The laws addressing the ramifications of drinking and driving change almost annually. This is true in no small part due to the constant pressure by MADD (Mothers Against Drunk Driving) on legislators to keep toughening up the laws regarding drunk drivers. Such laws are frequently revised and contain many interrelated crimes, which range from misdemeanors punishable by 93 days imprisonment to 20-year felonies.

Driving Under the Influence (DUI)

In many states, a person is guilty of DUI when that person (1) operates a motor vehicle on a highway or other place open to the general public or generally accessible to motor vehicles, and (2) is *either* under the influence of alcohol, a controlled substance, or a combination of alcohol and a controlled substance, and/or with an unlawful blood alcohol level of .08 grams or more.

Experienced criminal defense attorneys are often asked what constitutes "operating" a vehicle under the terms of the statute. The typical case is when a person is arrested for DUI after he or she was discovered by a police officer "sleeping it off" in the driver's seat of the vehicle. In this case, context is everything. A knowledgeable attorney will ask, "Was the car legally parked in a parking lot, or stopped on or beside a roadway?" "Was the key in the ignition?" "Was the engine running?" "Was there evidence that the person had actually been driving the vehicle?" The focus under the law is the danger that the intoxicated driver posed to the public based on the positioning of the vehicle, considering the facts and circumstances of each particular case. If the evidence tends to show that the person stumbled out of a bar after having too many drinks and decided to "sleep it off" in his car rather than drive home, then a conviction for DUI should never occur. If the person actually drove the vehicle for any amount of time, however, even to change parking spaces, then there is a strong potential for a conviction.

Another common question is whether a person whose blood alcohol level is under .08 can be convicted of DUI. Surprisingly, the answer is *yes*. This is because the DUI statute states that a driver is guilty of DUI if he or she *either* has a .08 or above blood alcohol level *or* was "under the influence of alcohol" when the driver operated the motor vehicle. As a practical matter, however, if the driver's blood alcohol level is less than .08 grams, if charges are authorized at all, the prosecutor will likely charge the driver with operating while visibly impaired, rather than DUI. But, again, it depends on the facts of the case.

In many states, a "motor vehicle is "every device in, upon, or by which any person or property is or may be transported or drawn upon a highway, except devices exclusively moved by human power or used exclusively upon stationary rails or tracks and except, only for the purpose of titling and registration under this act, a mobile home. It has been held that a bulldozer, dune buggy, and go-cart operated on the highway are all "motor vehicles" for the purposes of many states' drunk driving laws!

Surprisingly, a person can be arrested for DUI, not only for driving on a roadway, but also for driving in a parking lot or other place "generally accessible to motor vehicles," or a place that is "open to the general public." For example, the courts have held that a road in a trailer park was "open to the public" under the statute for the purposes of a DUI conviction.

In many states, a first-offense DUI is a misdemeanor punishable by up to 93 days in jail, a fine of $100–$500, and/or up to 360 hours of community service. Sanctions to your driver's license include a suspension for 30 days, and restrictions for an additional 150 days; possibly, six points will be added to your driving record, and you will owe a reinstatement fee of $1,000 for two consecutive years to keep your driver's license. The court is also permitted to immobilize the driver's motor vehicle for up to 180 days and could order an ignition interlock device be installed in your motor vehicle.

A second conviction for DUI within seven years of the first is a misdemeanor punishable by incarceration for a term from five days to one year, with not less than 48 hours to be served consecutively, a fine of $200–$1,000, and/or community service for 30 to 90 days. The court may forfeit the driver's vehicle, but if it chooses not to, then it *must* be immobilized for 90 to 180 days. Sanctions to your driver's license include a revocation for at least one year, plus six points added to your official driving record, and a reinstatement fee of $1,000 for two years to keep your driver's license. Additionally, in many states, there is a drivers' plate confiscation, possible vehicle forfeiture, and/or immobilization for 90 to 180 days.

A third conviction for DUI, regardless of how many years have passed since the prior convictions, is a felony punishable by one to five years imprisonment or probation with a jail term of 30 days to one year, with not less than 48 hours to be served consecutively. The court will order community service for 60 to 180 days and a fine of $500–$5,000, and may order vehicle forfeiture and/or license plate confiscation. If the court does not forfeit the vehicle, then it *must* be immobilized for one to three years.

Driver's License Suspension

As we stated earlier, in many states, sanctions to your driver's license include a suspension for 30 days, and restrictions for an additional 150 days. For these first 30 days, the offender cannot drive. This is known as a "hard suspension." Thereafter, the offender will have a "restricted license" to drive for the next 150 days. During the 150 days of having a restricted driver's license, the offender will be allowed to drive to, from, and in the course of work or school; to and from court-ordered services, such as counseling; and to and from regularly scheduled medical treatment, such as kidney dialysis.

In many states, persons under 21 years of age, who consume or purchase alcohol, face fines of between $100 and $500 (first, second, or third offense) with their driver's license being suspended for 30–60 days for second and third offenses under this statute, and for restrictions of an additional 60 days for a second offense and 305 days for a third offense.

Additional driver's license restrictions also apply for minors who transport or possess alcohol in motor vehicles and for motorists who drive while their license is suspended or who knowingly allow a person with a suspended license to drive a motor vehicle. There are also more severe penalties for drivers who endanger children by driving with children in their motor vehicles while intoxicated from alcohol or drugs. These are referred to as child endangerment cases.

Controlled Substance Crimes

Possession or Delivery of Marijuana

If you are arrested in a state in which Marijuana is still classified as a Schedule 1 controlled substance. A person who knowingly or intentionally possesses any amount of marijuana, and is not a registered medical marijuana patient or caregiver, is guilty of a misdemeanor punishable by up to one year in jail and a fine of not more than $1,000. There are also sanctions on the convicted person's driver's license. In many states, the statute does not make distinctions about the quantity of marijuana that the person possesses. Therefore, a person who possesses one gram and a person who possesses four grams can be charged with and convicted of the same possession crime. However, as a practical matter, the more marijuana in a person's possession, the more likely it is that the person will be charged with a much more serious crime, This is particularly true if the marijuana is found separated into smaller, individual bags, or if it is located near a scale or a cutter. Law enforcement personnel consider these signs that the person in possession of marijuana intends to deliver (or "sell") it to another person. In many states. This conviction ranges from a four-year felony to a 15-year felony, depending on the amount of marijuana (measured in kilograms or number of plants) the person has in his or her possession.

Use of Marijuana

In many states, marijuana is still illegal. A person who is not a registered Medical Marijuana patient, and is convicted of *using* marijuana, can be convicted of a misdemeanor punishable by up to 90 days in jail and a fine of up to $100. It seems to be illogical that a person could be charged or convicted of *using* marijuana without actually  *possessing* it, which is a separate crime. As a practical matter, however, the use of marijuana crime is a popular lesser offense that is utilized primarily for plea-bargaining purposes.

Maintaining a Drug House

In states where marijuana is still considered to be illegal, a person may not "knowingly keep or maintain a store, shop, warehouse, dwelling, building, vehicle, boat, aircraft, or other structure or place, that is frequented by persons using controlled substances. A conviction under this statute is a high court misdemeanor punishable by up to two years in prison and a fine of up to $25,000.

Use of a Schedule 1 or 2 Controlled Substance

In many states, a person who uses a Schedule 1 or 2 controlled substance, (except for marijuana) is guilty of a misdemeanor punishable by up to one year in jail and a fine of up to $2,000. Generally, Schedule 1 controlled substances are drugs that have a high potential for abuse but serve no legitimate medical purpose. Some examples of common Schedule 1 controlled substances include ecstasy (MDMA), LSD, and GHB (commonly known as the "date rape drug"). Schedule 2 controlled substances are drugs that have a high potential for abuse and addiction, but which have an approved medical use in the United States. These drugs include cocaine, hydrocodone, methadone, and methamphetamines.

Possession of a Schedule 1 or 2 Controlled Substance

In many states, a person who possesses a Schedule 1 or 2 controlled substance is guilty of anywhere from a four-year felony to a felony punishable by life in prison, depending on the amount of the substance of which the person is in possession. Possession of methamphetamine or ecstasy (MDMA), in any amount, is a felony punishable by up to 10 years in prison and a fine of up to $15,000.

Delivery or Manufacture of a Schedule 1 or 2 Controlled Substance

In many states, delivering or manufacturing a Schedule 1 or 2 controlled substance is a felony punishable by anywhere from seven years in prison up to life imprisonment, depending on the substance and the amount that the person delivers or manufactures.

Recently, there is a trend among college students to use Adderall as a recreational substance and to sell or share it with their friends. Adderall, which is commonly prescribed for Attention Deficit Hyperactivity Disorder (ADHD), is a combination of four amphetamine salts. Amphetamine, and its salts, are Schedule 2 controlled substances. Adderall is also a narcotic. Therefore, in many states, college students who possess small amounts of Adderall are guilty of four-year felonies. If they sell (or "deliver") Adderall to their classmates, they could be charged with a felony punishable by up to 20 years in prison! Accordingly, sharing an Adderall pill with a college student during exam time is very risky business and should never be done.

Many people do not realize that controlled substance offenses also carry driver's license sanctions, regardless of whether the offense involved operating a motor vehicle. In many states, a person convicted of a controlled substance violation faces a mandatory six-month suspension of their operating privileges. The sentencing judge may allow a restricted license, but only after 30 days of full suspension. On a second conviction, the suspension becomes one year, with the possibility of a restricted license after 60 days.

Minor Traffic Offenses

Traffic offenses come in two varieties: civil infractions and criminal offenses. Generally, a civil infraction is "an act or omission prohibited by law which is not a crime . . . and for which civil sanctions may be ordered. In contrast, a crime is "an act or omission forbidden by law which is not designated as a civil infraction, and which is punishable upon conviction by any 1 or more of the following: (a) Imprisonment. (b) Fine not designated a civil fine. (c) Removal from office. (d) Disqualification to hold an office of trust, honor, or profit under the state. (e) Other penal discipline". A civil infraction is not a crime, and an arrest warrant cannot be issued if a person is only charged with a civil infraction. However, if the person who has been issued a civil infraction fails to appear or otherwise respond to any pending matter related to the civil infraction action (failure to do so is a misdemeanor), then the court will notify the Secretary of State (SOS), who will suspend the person's driver's license. If the person is later stopped while driving on a suspended driver's license, which is a misdemeanor, then the court may issue an arrest warrant.

The district court, and any municipal court, has jurisdiction over traffic civil infraction actions. In many states, some courts have district court traffic bureaus that handle such cases. These district courts may also permit a magistrate to preside over some civil infraction actions.

Equipment Violations

Many states have a law that requires that all motor vehicles have the correct and operable equipment when driven on road-ways. This includes lighting equipment, brakes, mirrors, windshields and windshield wipers, horns and other warning devices, muffler and exhaust systems, tires, etc.. Many equipment violations are civil infractions that add no points to the driver's license and have a minor fine.

Careless Driving

In many states, the law states that a "person who operates a vehicle upon a highway or a frozen public lake, stream, or pond or other place open to the general public including an area designated for the parking of vehicles in a careless or negligent manner likely to endanger any person or property, but without wantonness or recklessness, is responsible for a civil infraction" In many states, careless driving is a civil infraction that adds three points to the driver's license and carries a small fine.

Driving without Proof of Insurance

A person who operates a motor vehicle on a roadway must carry proof of the vehicle's insurance at all times. Failure to do so is a civil infraction that carries no driver's license points. If the driver provides proof to the court that he or she has insurance prior to the appearance date on the citation, then the court will not assess a fine or costs or abstract the matter to the SOS, and the court can assess a fee of not more than $25. Under some circumstances, the court can require the driver to surrender his driver's license and suspend it. Although, until recently, in many states, the law requires a $200 per year driver responsibility fee for two years, there no longer is such a requirement for a violation of this statute.

Criminal Traffic Offenses

Leaving the Scene of an Accident

Under the law of many states, vehicle accidents require that the operator of the vehicle take some affirmative steps after the crash. Whether it is a single-car or multiple-car accident, it is always best to stop and identify yourself, if it can be done safely.

Vehicle codes usually require a driver of a vehicle, who knows or has reason to believe that they have been involved in an accident, to immediately stop his or her vehicle at the scene and do the following:

- Provide his or her name, address, and the registration number of his or her vehicle, as well as the name and address of the actual owner of the motor vehicle to a police officer, the person struck, or occupants of the other vehicle.

- Display his or her driver's license to a police officer, the individual struck, or occupants of the other vehicle.

- Reasonably help anyone injured get aid or transportation.

Should a driver have a reasonable and honest belief that remaining at the scene will result in *further harm*, he or she is required to immediately report the accident to the nearest or many convenient police officer.

In many states, failure to do the above can result in being charged with a misdemeanor punishable by up to 90 days in jail, fines, and costs. If there is injury to any person, the offender's punishment could be increased to a full year in jail and fines of $1,000 plus costs, together with a license suspension.

All of the serious criminal traffic offenses below provide that the driver shall receive six points on their driving record, and incur a driver responsibility fee of $1,000 per year for two years.

In the following paragraphs, charges/convictions are likely to include these sanctions:

Driving Under the Influence Due to the Use of Alcohol or Drugs Causing Death

Penalties: Felony, imprisonment up to 15 years and/or a fine of $2,500–$10,000.

Sanctions: Driving license revoked for a minimum of one year, license plate confiscated, and vehicle required to be immobilized up to 180 days.

Driving on a Suspended License Causing Death

Penalties: Felony, imprisonment up to 15 years and/or a fine of $2,500–$10,000.

Sanctions: Driving license revoked for a minimum of one year, license plate confiscated, and vehicle immobilized for up to 180 days, if not forfeited.

Driving While License Suspended Causing Serious Impairment of a Body Function

Penalties: Felony, imprisonment up to five years and/or a fine of $1,000–$5,000.

Sanctions: Driver license minimum of one-year revocation/denial, license plate required to be confiscated, immobilization of vehicle required up to 180 days unless forfeited.

Moving Violation Causing Death

Penalties: Misdemeanor, jail incarceration for up to one year and/or fine of up to $2,000.

Sanctions: Mandatory one-year license suspension.

Civil Infraction Causing Serious Impairment of a Body Function

Common Criminal Charges

Penalties: Misdemeanor, providing for jail incarceration for up to 93 days and/or fine of up to $500.

Sanctions: Mandatory one-year license suspension.

7

THE JUDICIAL PROCESS

When a police officer believes that a crime has been committed in his or her presence, or the officer has "probable cause" to believe that a felony (or one of a certain type of misdemeanor) was committed that the officer did not personally witness, the officer may arrest the suspect on the spot, without an arrest warrant. Later, the police officer will submit a warrant request to the prosecutor, requesting that potential charges be authorized.

It is important for all individuals charged with a crime, to understand the role of the prosecuting attorney. Therefore, in the following paragraphs, I will describe the process that occurs in many states.

Generally, unless the prosecutor has reviewed a search warrant earlier in the case, the prosecutor's involvement with a case begins when the investigating officer requests a warrant. This is the point at which the prosecutor determines whether a person should be charged with a crime and, if so, what the crime will be. The prosecutor will review the police report and all of the available records in the case. This includes statements made by witnesses and the suspect, if he or she has chosen to make any. The prosecutor also will take a look at the suspect's prior criminal history and driving record. The prosecutor can issue a charge if he or she believes that there is probable cause to believe that the suspect committed a crime. Once the prosecutor authorizes the warrant, the suspect will be arrested, if he or she is not already in custody.

The First Court Appearance

The first court appearance for someone charged with a crime is the arraignment. At that point, the person suspected of the crime is classified in the court system as a "defendant." At the arraignment, the magistrate or district court judge informs the defendant of the charges against him or her, including the maximum penalty, if convicted. The magistrate or judge also reads the defendant his or her rights, including the right to a trial by judge or jury, the right to court-appointed counsel, and the presumption that the suspect is innocent until proven guilty.

Setting a Bond

Bond is usually set at the arraignment after a person is arrested and taken to jail. Outstanding warrants may have already had the bond set such that when he or she is arrested they can post a specific amount of money as their bond (e.g., for back child support).

The magistrate, or judge, will set the bond in the case. The amount of the bond will vary depending on the seriousness of the allegations in the matter. A defendant charged with a low-level misdemeanor, for example, may receive a "personal recognizance" bond. This means that the defendant will not need to post a monetary bond in order to remain free from jail. In contrast, a defendant charged with a more serious felony will be expected to post a more sizeable bond. Often the judge or magistrate will impose conditions on the bond, such as requiring the defendant not to have contact with an alleged victim or not to consume alcohol while the case is pending.

At this point, the pretrial judicial process varies, depending on whether the defendant is charged with a misdemeanor or a felony. If the defendant is charged with a misdemeanor, the magistrate or judge will expect him or her to enter a plea of "guilty" or "not guilty." If the defendant pleads guilty (or "no contest"), the judge may sentence the defendant at that time or may reschedule the case for another sentencing date in order to give the probation department time to write a presentence report. If the defendant pleads "not guilty," or stands mute and does not enter a plea, the judge or magistrate will set the case for a pretrial or settlement conference with the prosecutor. If the defendant requests a court-appointed attorney, one may be appointed at that time.

A settlement or pretrial conference is scheduled in every misdemeanor case. This is a meeting between the defendant (or his or her attorney) and an assistant prosecutor. The goal of the meeting is to determine whether the case will be resolved by a plea or whether a trial will be necessary. If the prosecutor will be offering a plea bargain, the offer is usually made at the settlement conference. Many of the time a judge is not present for this meeting.

If the defendant is charged with a felony, the defendant does not enter a plea at the initial arraignment in district court. Instead, under newly enacted legislation, the district court judge will schedule a date and time for a probable cause conference between seven and 14 days after the arraignment and also schedule a date and time for a preliminary examination between five and seven days after the date of the scheduled probable cause conference. If the defendant requests a court-appointed attorney, one may be appointed at that time.

Guilty Until Proven Innocent

At the probable cause conference, the defendant's attorney and the prosecutor will discuss the legal and factual issues of the case and determine whether a preliminary examination will be held in the case. The prosecutor likely will make an initial plea offer at the probable cause conference. If the defendant chooses to waive his or her right to a preliminary examination, and if the prosecutor agrees, there will be no preliminary examination conducted. On the other hand, if the defendant chooses to have a preliminary examination, many prosecutors will consider any plea agreement offered to be "revoked," and any plea offer will no longer be available to the defendant unless the preliminary examination outcome is favorable to the defendant.

A preliminary examination is a basic evidentiary hearing during which the prosecutor must only prove to the judge that there is "probable cause" to believe that the charged crime was committed, and that the defendant is the person who committed the crime. The burden of proof is much less than a trial, so generally the prosecutor will call only a few witnesses to testify. Usually this includes only the alleged victim, the police witnesses, and perhaps additional eyewitnesses to the matter, if any. The defendant, through his or her attorney, can cross-examine the witnesses and present his own witnesses. As a practical matter, however, the defense rarely produces evidence at this hearing, in order to avoid "tipping his or her hand" to the prosecutor prior to trial. Unless the criminal defense attorney believes he or she can prevent the case from being "bound over" to circuit court, many defense attorneys will waive conducting the preliminary examination. Reasons to conduct a preliminary examination include:

1. to pursue evidence (all witnesses),

2. to nail down the stories of witnesses, and

3. to preserve the testimony of a witness who might be unavailable at the trial.

If the judge decides that there is probable cause that the defendant committed the charged crime, the judge will order the matter "bound over" to circuit court for trial. The defendant will be arraigned again, be advised of his or her constitutional rights, and enter a plea to the charge. The available pleas are "guilty," "not guilty," "nolle contendre," or "stand mute." An accused can enter a "nolle contendre" plea (which has the same practical effect as entering a "guilty" plea) when there is the possibility of a civil action arising out of the same incident, or when the accused has no recollection of the events surrounding the incident due to memory loss (i.e., when a party is involved in an auto accident causing a traumatic brain injury or memory loss due to intoxication or being in shock). When a defendant "stands mute," as opposed to *pleading* "not guilty," an accused is legally stating, "I'm not even admitting you have jurisdiction over me regarding the charges brought against me." Accordingly, by "standing mute" an accused does not waive any jurisdictional defects in his or her case. If the defendant chooses to "stand mute," then a not guilty plea will be entered on his or her behalf. Often, at that point another settlement conference between the prosecutor and the defense attorney is scheduled in the matter.

Testing the Evidence

Whether the case is a felony or a misdemeanor, if it is not resolved with a plea agreement during the settlement or pretrial conference, it might be necessary to file "motions" in the case. A pretrial motion is the method by which the judge is presented with issues that are in dispute in the case. Pretrial motions generally deal with legal or constitutional issues, such as whether a defendant's statement is admissible into evidence against him, or whether the search of a defendant's home or vehicle was constitutionally valid. If the only issues in the case are factual, such as whether the defendant actually committed the acts that he is accused of doing, then pretrial motions are generally not appropriate and the matter must be decided by a jury. This is because the judge is in charge of deciding the law that applies to every case, but the jury is in charge of deciding what facts occurred in every case.

After the pretrial motions have been decided by the judge, there is usually an opportunity for the defendant to enter a plea prior to trial. However, if the defendant has turned down the initial plea offer in order to take his or her chances with motions before the judge, then the original plea offer may no longer be available. If the defendant's motions were successful (such as a "motion to suppress evidence"), then the plea offer may be better than the original offer. However, if the defendant's motions did not succeed, it is likely that the plea offer made by the prosecutor at that time will be substantially worse.

A trial is an adversarial proceeding during which the prosecutor has the burden of proving that the defendant is guilty "beyond a reasonable doubt" of the crime(s) with which he or she is charged. The prosecutor must present evidence, but the defendant is not required to prove his or her innocence in any way. As a practical matter, however, the defense presents evidence in almost every trial. Evidence can take many forms, including the testimony of witnesses, experts, lab reports, and much more. The scope of the evidence is limited only by the states' Rules of Evidence, with which each party is expected to comply. This is true even if the defendant is representing himself or herself and does not have an attorney.

The prosecutor and the defendant each have the right to a trial by jury. However, if the parties agree that the trial will be heard by a judge without a jury (known as a "bench"

1-888-888-6582

trial), the court may allow it. In a trial by jury, the jury is the "decider of fact." In a bench trial, the judge decides the facts of the case.

Sentencing

If the defendant enters a guilty plea or is convicted after trial, he or she will be sentenced by the judge. The sentencing procedure varies depending on whether the defendant is being sentenced for a felony or a misdemeanor. In many counties, before a defendant is sentenced on a misdemeanor, the judge will refer the case to the probation office in order to write a "pre-sentence" report that includes information about the crime, the defendant's personal background and criminal history, and a statement by the victim if one is available. In many states, all felony sentencing "pre-sentencing reports", are written by the Department of Corrections. Although the information in the pre-sentence report is subject to factual challenges by the parties, the contents of the pre-sentence report are usually taken very seriously by the judge when considering the defendant's sentence. The judge considers the pre-sentence report, together with evidence presented by both parties, statements of the defendant and any victim, and other information relevant to the sentencing decision. In felony sentences, in many cases, the judge must sentence the defendant within his or her "sentencing guidelines." The judge must also order restitution to the victim, if applicable.

However, upon request, the defendant is entitled to a separate hearing as to the amount of restitution.

Youthful Offenders

Depending on the type of case, there are options available for delaying or deferring sentences. For example, defendants who plead guilty to an offense that was committed after their 17th birthday, but before they turned 21 years old, may qualify for a deferral. Additionally, a defendant who enters a plea to certain drug offenses may also qualify for a deferral. Additionally, as discussed previously, a defendant who enters a plea to a first offense of domestic violence may qualify for a deferral.

All of these options allow a defendant to avoid having a public conviction on his or her record. However, as previously stated, in many states, the law was recently changed to allow convictions that were deferred and

dismissed under the domestic violence deferral to count as a prior conviction for purposes of enhanced sentencing. This means this deferral cannot be expunged. Moreover, there is no guarantee that in the future, many state laws won't be similarly changed to allow drug-related deferrals to be used to enhance "second-offense" convictions. Therefore, a plea with a delayed or deferred status is not to be taken lightly and should only be done with advice of counsel.

8

HOW A CONVICTION CAN RUIN YOUR LIFE

When an individual is charged with a criminal offense, both attorneys and offenders tend to focus on the more obvious and immediate effect of a conviction: incarceration—the length of time and place of incarceration (local jail or prison). Offenders think, "Am I going to go to jail or prison?" Attorneys think, "How can I get my client's charge(s) reduced to keep my client doing as little jail or prison time as possible?" Sadly, this tunnel-vision approach often leads to clients, and occasionally their attorneys,

How a Conviction Can Ruin Your Life

acting too quickly and overlooking major collateral consequences of a conviction that are in addition to incarceration and the statutory fines and sentence imposed.

Collateral consequences of a conviction, in simplest terms, are those consequences that extend beyond incarceration and fines and costs. For example, many people would gladly accept a plea offer that reduces their felony drug charge down to a misdemeanor, without considering that such a conviction may also carry with it a driver's license sanction that could cost them their job. In many states, sentencing guidelines largely control how much time a convicted client is going to spend behind bars, but there are many other things that will also affect the client when they get out of jail or prison. A person's ability to vote or carry a weapon may be forfeited. Some parents might lose custody of their children, while others may find it difficult to obtain employment, or state or federal aid.

The topic of the collateral consequences of a criminal conviction could easily fill pages of an entire book. However, this chapter will only cover some of the many common and serious collateral consequences of convictions for specific crimes. Remember, it's important to talk to an experienced criminal defense attorney to know what other possible consequences your conviction may cause.

Driver's License Sanctions

Many people realize that if they are charged with a driving offense, such as driving under the influence, they will have some sort of driver's license sanction. Driver's license sanctions, however, can be imposed in convictions for several non-driving-related offenses.

In many states, the courts are required to abstract to the Secretary of State certain convictions that require the Secretary of State to impose license sanctions for drug convictions, regardless of whether you were driving a motor vehicle when your offense occurred. For example, in states where marijuana is still illegal, upon a first offense of possession of marijuana you could receive a license suspension for six months. In such a case, the court could issue a restricted license after 30 days—similar to a first offense of driving under the influence. A second conviction for possession of marijuana calls for a one-year suspension. With a second conviction, the court could grant a restricted license after 60 days. In many states, these license sanctions are waived when a defendant is sentenced to more than one year in jail or prison.

Many state legislatures enacted these driver's license sanctions as a way to deter people from committing drug crimes by having drug offenses carry stiffer penalties.

However, since the citizens of many states don't know about the driver license sanction consequences, their effect as a deterrent is questionable.

Commercial Driver's License Sanctions

A commercial driver's license comes with significantly more responsibility than a standard operator's license. As such, commercial drivers are subject to much stricter rules and regulations. A person who possesses a commercial driver's license is at risk of losing that license when they commit criminal offenses while driving their personal vehicles. For example, if you are convicted of a drunk driving offense in your personal vehicle, you will also lose your commercial driver's license for not less than one year.

Employment

Certain occupations require special licenses to maintain employment. If your profession is governed by any kind of oversight committee, a criminal conviction could have a drastic impact on your ability to continue earning a living from your profession. It's imperative that you discuss any special licenses with your criminal defense attorney at the outset of your case to best manage any impact that a conviction for a particular crime might have. Knowing the consequences of a conviction can also give your attorney options when negotiating for a plea bargain in your case.

1-888-888-6582

For a comprehensive list of the occupations regulated under your state's Occupational Code, refer to the State of . . . website. The following is a list of professions and occupations that are regulated by the Bureau of Health Care Services:

- acupuncture
- athletic trainer
- audiologist
- chiropractic
- counseling
- dentistry
- dietetics and nutrition
- marriage and family therapy
- massage therapy
- medicine
- nurse aide
- nursing
- nursing home administrator
- occupational therapy
- optometry
- osteopathic medicine and surgery
- pharmacy
- physical therapy
- physician's assistant
- podiatric medicine and surgery
- psychology

- respiratory care
- sanitarian
- social worker
- speech language pathology
- veterinarian

In many states, these professions are subject to the rules and regulations of the Public Health Code. The Public Health Code lists specific convictions that could trigger an investigation and possible disciplinary action for anyone who holds a license under the code. These crimes range from a misdemeanor conviction that is reasonably related to, or adversely affects, the licensee's ability to practice in a safe and competent manner, to convictions for much more serious felonies such as criminal sexual conduct in the first degree.

Additionally, in many states, a licensee must notify the Department of Licensing and Regulatory Affairs of *any* criminal conviction within 30 days after the date of the conviction. Failure to make the required notification will likely result in an investigation and disciplinary action. If you have been charged with a crime, it's important to know how a possible conviction will impact your licensee status.

Financial Aid

If you are a student currently receiving Federal Student Aid or plan to apply for Federal Student Aid in the near future, it is important to understand how certain convictions may affect your eligibility to receive aid.

A conviction for a drug-related offense will have the greatest impact on your ability to receive Federal Student Aid. The timing of the conviction is also very important. If you are receiving financial aid when you are convicted of either possessing or selling a controlled substance, your eligibility to continue to receive aid may be suspended. When you complete your Free Application for Federal Student Aid (FAFSA) you will be asked whether you have had a drug conviction while receiving aid. Answering the question in the affirmative will require you to fill out additional paperwork about your conviction.

If your conviction results in your inability to receive financial aid, you can regain that privilege by successfully completing an approved drug rehabilitation program or by passing two random drug screens administered by an approved drug rehabilitation program. Perhaps more important to note, if you are convicted of a drug-related offense after you have submitted your application for Federal Student Aid, you may be held liable for returning any funds you received during a period of ineligibility.

Deportation and International Travel

Students and other visitors to America who have visas could face deportation upon conviction for crimes involving moral turpitude and other specified crimes. Individuals convicted for driving under the influence of alcohol or drugs, or driving while impaired due to the use of alcohol or drugs, will learn that such convictions may bar them from travel across the border from the United States to Canada. At the time of this writing, Canada considers such motor vehicle crimes "to be serious criminal offenses" barring entry into their country, even though such offenses may be considered to be misdemeanors in many states. The rules for entering Canada with a DUI on your record are being continually updated. Do research on the internet to be informed of the most recent laws governing DUI's and travel to other countries.

A person with a conviction for DUI may, after a period of time, be considered "rehabilitated" and eligible for entry into other countries. Time periods vary for particular offenses and the time does not begin to run until after completion of the sentence imposed. Other options may be available to offenders to rehabilitate themselves, and those concerned with how their conviction might affect their ability to travel outside of the United States should seek advice from an experienced criminal defense attorney.

Guilty Until Proven Innocent

Child Support

If you are obligated to make payments under a child support order, and you have committed a crime that could result in your incarceration for any extended period of time, you need to know that your child support obligation will not be suspended during your incarceration, *unless* you notify the family law court of your incarceration. This process is known as *tolling* your support obligation. Failing to do this could cost you dearly. For example, if your child support obligation is $200 a month and you are sentenced to five years in prison, you will owe $12,000 upon your release, and this amount *cannot* be forgiven once you have incured it.

9

Expunging Convictions

If you have ever been convicted of a crime, you know that it can have a big impact on your life. Even if the conviction occurred many years ago, employers can use your criminal record as a reason not to hire or promote you in your job. Additionally, a criminal conviction can make you ineligible for certain types of government housing programs and unappealing to potential landlords. The conviction can also make you ineligible for federal student loans and government benefits, and can influence your immigration status if you are not a United States citizen. For these reasons, it is always best to have your criminal conviction set aside (or "expunged") if possible.

Many Types of Convictions Can Be Expunged

In many states, the law allows many criminal convictions to be set aside. There are a few exceptions, however. For example, if your conviction is for a felony or an attempted felony for which the maximum punishment is life in prison, such as first-degree murder, then the conviction cannot be set aside. Similarly, if you have been convicted of criminal sexual conduct (CSC) as an adult, then the conviction cannot be expunged. Likewise, if you have been convicted of a misdemeanor traffic offense, such as drunk driving, driving without a license, or any other criminal misdemeanor under most states Vehicle Code, you are not eligible to have your conviction set aside. If your conviction is for a non-traffic offense that is reportable to the Secretary of State, such as for a drug offense, the court cannot order its removal from your driving record even if your record is expunged.

Only One Expungement, with One Big Exception

Generally, the court will only set aside one conviction, and that conviction must be the only one on your criminal record. You cannot have more than one conviction expunged, even if the convictions arose from the same criminal transaction and they occurred on the same date. For example, if you were convicted of assault and battery, a 93-day misdemeanor, and interfering with electronic communications, a two-year felony, based on an incident that occurred on the same date at the same time, then you cannot ask the court to set aside either or both of those convictions. Generally, you cannot have more than one conviction on your record at the time that you ask for the expungement.

In some states, there is an exception to the "one conviction" rule. It may be possible to ask the court to have a conviction expunged if you have a total of three convictions on your record, but not more than two of them are "minor offenses" that occurred before you turned 21 years of age. For example, suppose you also were originally convicted of aggravated assault, a one-year misdemeanor, when you were 25 years of age. However, when you were a 20-year-old college student, you picked up convictions for attending a nuisance party and disturbing the peace, both of which are 90-day misdemeanors. You may still be eligible to ask the court to set aside your conviction for aggravated assault, despite the fact that you have the two "minor convictions" on your record from your college years.

You Must Wait at Least Five Years

Even if you are otherwise eligible to have your conviction set aside, you may not ask the court to expunge your conviction until five years have passed since the date that the sentence was imposed or you were released from incarceration, whichever is later. For example, if, on January 1, 2009, you were convicted of maintaining a drug house and sentenced to a jail term of 12 months, you must wait until at least January 1, 2015, to ask the court to set aside your conviction.

Juvenile Adjudications

There is a common myth that a person's juvenile criminal history disappears from his or her record when that person becomes an adult. However, unless the juvenile convictions (or "adjudications," as they are known in the court system) were pursuant to a specific agreement, sometimes referred to as an informal or "consent" calendar, that is not the case. Unless the person specifically asks the court to set aside those juvenile adjudications (or "expunge" them), the person's juvenile record will remain on their criminal history forever.

In many cases, a person's juvenile criminal history is readily available to anyone doing a criminal background check. This can include prospective employers, educational institutions, and media outlets. In fact, many states have a law that provides that portions of juvenile court files are public records, open for inspection by anyone for any purpose.

Many people with juvenile criminal records should seriously consider having their adjudications expunged. Many state legislatures have recently amended the Juvenile Expungement Statute of their state to expand the number of offenses that may be expunged from a person's criminal record. Now, if allowed by the states' laws, a person may be able to seek to set aside up to three juvenile offenses, of which only one may be the equivalent of a felony if it were committed as an adult. This is true only if the person does not have any adult convictions for felonies at the time that he or she seeks to expunge the juvenile adjudications.

Many juvenile adjudications are eligible to be set aside. The only exceptions include adjudications that would be life offenses if they had been committed as an adult, traffic offenses, and adjudications for an offense for which the juvenile was tried and convicted as an adult. A person can ask the court to set aside his or her juvenile adjudications after one year has passed since the disposition of the matter or the person's release from juvenile detention, or after the person turns 18 years of age, whichever is later.

The expungement process is a complicated one and requires a court hearing at which the prosecutor likely will be present. An experienced criminal defense attorney can guide you through the process of setting aside your juvenile criminal history and putting your youthful mistakes behind you.

10

WHEN YOU ARE CHARGED OR SUSPECTED OF CRIME

How to Make Sure You Get the Best Criminal Defense Attorney to Protect Your Rights

1. Contact people you respect in the jurisdiction where you've been charged and ask for their opinion. References from other lawyers who practice in the area where you've been charged or from friends and acquaintances who have had experience with other lawyers can often be very helpful. Also, checking on a reputable website that ranks attorneys in various practice areas can also be extremely helpful. Two sites that I recommend are www.avvo.com and www.martindale.com. These websites help people find lawyers. For example, someone could use www.avvo.com to search for a criminal defense attorney in Los Angeles, California. These services also review whether there has been any disciplinary action by the State Bar of California against an attorney. These search engines rely on lawyers familiar with the attorney and past clients of the attorney to rate the attorney based on his or her abilities and past experiences with clients. Importantly, knowing whether an attorney has had previous ethical problems when representing another client should be a red flag for hiring such an individual.

2. *Contact police officers and individuals who work in law enforcement.* Surprisingly, many people in the local courthouse will be open and tell you who they think "is the best criminal defense lawyer" to handle your criminal case (even if it's a police officer who has been asked to make a recommendation!). My suggestion is to politely ask around at the courthouse; talk to people who regularly work in the courtroom, such as bailiffs and clerks. Simply ask, "If you were charged with a crime, which lawyer in this county would you recommend? Who do you think might help me if I had to try my case?" There's a difference between a lawyer who can walk you through the system and plead you guilty, and a lawyer who can look into the souls of jurors and tell them that he or she is your lawyer and is here to prove your innocence. When deciding upon a name for this book, it's no accident that I selected the title *Guilty Until Proven Innocent*. Nowadays, especially with CSI

afoot, jurors expect the defense attorney to prove that their client did not commit the crime. You need to hire an aggressive attorney who not only talks the tough talk, but who also has a track record of going to court and winning. You need to make sure that you hire an attorney to represent you who is willing to work hard *preparing* to go to trial, if necessary, and has done so a number of times with successful results.

3. *Select an attorney who regularly practices before the courts in the jurisdiction where you have been charged.* If you are from San Diego, but charged in Pasadena, it's normally not advisable for you to hire a San Diego attorney to represent you in your case in.Pasadena. Conversely, if you are from Pasadena, but charged with a crime in San Diego County, my best advice is to hire the best criminal defense attorney you can afford who regularly tries criminal cases in San Diego   County.

If you have been arrested in an area that you are not familiar with, you can contact a good criminal defense attorney in the area where you live, and he or she will usually be helpful and do their best to refer you to an excellent criminal defense attorney in the area where you have been charged. I recommend that the best criminal defense attorney for you is *usually* someone who knows the local procedures and policies of police departments, prosecutors, and courts (as opposed to an out-of-area lawyer coming in and trying to work with people and procedures that he or she is not familiar with when trying to help you).

4. *Take a look at the potential attorney's experience level as evidenced by his or her number of years in practice, membership in professional affiliations, and background.* Was the defense attorney previously an assistant prosecuting attorney, or even a prosecuting attorney? If so, they will know both sides of the criminal justice system better than an individual who has only practiced criminal defense. Is he or she a member of a criminal defense attorney association. Such membership helps keep criminal defense attorneys up to date on the latest changes in criminal justice laws.

5. *Is the criminal defense attorney whom you are considering backed up by a team of professionals who work with him or her?* Many experienced criminal defense attorneys need to have at least one associate to help them with their cases and at least one or two paralegals to perform the necessary backup work to prep every case. It's difficult to rely on just one attorney to perform all of the functions that are necessary for a good criminal defense. What would happen if that one

attorney got sick or was unavailable when you many needed them? That's why, from my perspective, I believe having a legal team available to represent you is a better way to go. It also utilizes the maxim that two or three heads are better than just one when analyzing all of the legal issues that are unique to your particular case.

6. *Has the criminal defense attorney whom you are considering published any authoritative literary works focusing on their state's criminal justice system?* Obviously, it has been my experience that an individual who is willing to put his or her knowledge and experience into print to help advise others is usually more reliable when it comes to his or her credibility with the courts and the prosecutors' offices with whom he or she interacts on a regular basis.

7. *It's my recommendation that great lawyers in the courtroom typically are lawyers who also did well in their educational years.* While it's not always the case, if a lawyer struggled academically in undergraduate and in law school, the chances are remote that he or she will suddenly become brilliant in the courtroom. It's for that reason that a review of how the lawyer you are considering performed, at least in law school, might be of help when making your final decision as to which lawyer you want to trust with your case.

8. There is an old maxim: *you get what you pay for.* Lawyers who don't charge much for their legal services typically don't provide much service either. My advice is that you should hire a legal team with the understanding that the firm's number one trial lawyer will be the lawyer to try your criminal case, if necessary. But having an experienced legal team available to help you typically *does* cost more than just relying on one lawyer, who may or may not be available when you need to talk to him or her to help and to answer your questions.

One of the complaints many often voiced by clients who have hired a lawyer is that they can never connect with their lawyer, or "My lawyer never calls me back." When you have questions, and you have hired a legal team at a law firm, there is almost always someone from your legal team available to assist you who knows the ins and outs of your particular case. That is not the case when you've hired just one lawyer "for a flat fee" who may be on vacation when you need him or her. Make sure whichever lawyer you are considering hiring has a written fee agreement that explains any "engagement fee" or "minimum fee" that is charged, and that it provides a clear explanation of what the cost will be to you, on an hourly basis or otherwise, to resolve your case or should your matter proceed to trial.

While some attorneys do charge a flat fee, it is the experience of this author that a flat fee is seldom in the client's best interest. Do you want an attorney who is motivated to cut a deal and settle your case as fast as possible, or do you want an attorney who is motivated to get you the absolute best possible result and in doing so overlooks nothing? As an example, in a drunk driving case, are you going to hire a lawyer who takes the time to go and inspect the breath analyzer to make sure that it has been calibrated on a weekly basis, and every 120 days by a Class 4 Operator? When looking at a .08 or .09 blood alcohol content (BAC), this can be absolutely critical. At the jail, there are logs that are required to be maintained that confirm whether the breath analyzer is functioning properly. Such logs need to be personally verified if you are going to trial.

11

EPILOGUE

This book was written to help inform citizens of their rights under many states' criminal justice system. The author stresses that many police officers and prosecutors do an excellent job, day in and day out.

As stated in the Introduction, however, individuals with power are capable of abusing that power and wrongfully charging individuals with crimes they did not commit. There are also occasions when "witnesses" either lie or are mistaken (they thought they saw things that did not happen, or they thought they heard people say things that were not said). Accordingly, "evidence" may not be evidence at all, and partial truths may lead to erroneous conclusions causing innocent persons to be charged with crimes.

That is why having the assistance of an experienced criminal defense attorney can make all the difference in the world to the individual wrongfully charged. Even when someone has committed a criminal offense, often circumstances that led to the commission of the crime can make a huge difference on the outcome of the individual's case. Such circumstances, when properly explained by the individual's criminal defense attorney, may cause the prosecutor or sentencing judge to take a completely different approach when sanctioning the individual for his or her actions. This occurs when individuals are allowed to plea to lesser charges, or receive deferrals, delays, or caps in sentencing.

APPENDIX

INVOKING YOUR RIGHTS

If you are confronted by the police, who detain you for "questioning," here is a statement you can read to the police. This will help protect you from making incriminating statements, or from a claim that you consented to a search of your person, home, motor vehicle, or items of property in your possession (your purse, briefcase, etc.).

Appendix – Invoking Your Rights

"I hereby invoke and refuse to waive all of the following rights and privileges afforded to me by the U.S. Constitution:

- I invoke and refuse to waive my Fifth Amendment right to remain silent. Please do not ask me any questions.

- I invoke and refuse to waive my Sixth Amendment right to an attorney of my choice. Please do not ask me any questions without my attorney present.

- I invoke and refuse to waive all privileges and rights pursuant to the United States Supreme Court case, *Miranda v Arizona*. Please do not ask me any questions or make any comment to me about this decision.

- I invoke and refuse to waive my Fourth Amendment right to be free from unreasonable searches and seizures. I do not consent to any search or seizure of myself, my home, my motor vehicle, or of any property in my possession. Please do not ask me about my ownership interest in any property. I do not consent to this contact with you. If I am not presently under arrest or under investigatory detention, please allow me to leave.

- Any statement I make, or alleged consent I give, in response to your questions is hereby made under protest and under duress and in submission to your claim of lawful authority to force me to provide you with information."

IMPORTANT DISCLAIMER

This is an informational consumer guide intended to assist the public. It is not legal advice. It is written as general information and is not a substitute for informed legal, psychiatric, psychological, counseling, or other professional advice. Laws change; court decisions interpreting and changing case precedent occur weekly. All of these changes can cause advice to change as well, even advice based on the same or similar facts.

Some observant readers may come across a fact or two that might appear to be in error. They may consider writing me to point out such observations. In our world, my advice is we should all try to save trees (paper). There are mistakes in this book, as with many books. No matter how hard one tries to avoid mistakes—mistakes will always occur. My hope is that such unintended errors will be insignificant in nature, and that those observant readers finding errors will be both understanding and forgiving.

Accordingly, comments and opinions set forth in this book should not be relied on as legal advice, nor professional advice of any kind. Reading this book does not create an attorney/client relationship between the author and the reader. In order to receive proper legal advice or professional advice of any kind, an individual needs to discuss his or her unique facts with a professional who, *at that time*, will then

Disclaimer

be in a position to give the client their best professional advice.

ABOUT THE AUTHOR

Vincent W Davis Esq.

Mr. Davis obtained is Bachelor of Science degree in Accounting from Loyola Marymount University and his Juris Doctorate from Loyola Law School of Southern California.

Mr. Davis has been a member of the California State Bar since December 1986.

Mr. Davis is also eligible to practice law before the United States District Court for the Central District of California; the United States District Court of Appeals for the 9th Circuit and the Supreme Court of the United States.

Mr. Davis acted as both trial and appellate counsel in the published cases of: Marriage of David and Martha M., (2006) 140 Cal.App.4th 96 and Papakosmas v. Papakosmas, (2007) 483 F.3d 617.

On January 8, 2008, Mr. Davis received a diploma from the National Institute for Trial Advocacy. In 2008, he became a member of the Ranch Club- Trial Lawyers College. He was one of 50 lawyers selected nationwide to live, for 22 days on Gerry Spence's Thunderhead Ranch just outside of Dubois, Wyoming.